'Ante is an alchemical wonder of a poet: unparalleled in her image-making, raw to both historical and contemporary damage and rich in cultures. Utterly original, *AGIMAT* is itself a talisman – a fiery binding of pain and a message of love to the wounded and lost. Keep these poems with you as I will – always'
Fiona Benson

'If translation is always physical, often joyous work – the act of carrying meaning across the chasms separating languages – then *AGIMAT* is about the daily embodied acts involved in this labour. To live in translation is to be estranged. Yet the joy of translation comes from this very estrangement. Romalyn Ante makes us feel this, as estrangement transforms into its own vibrant space of joy. Ante's irrepressible inquiries into translation create a colourful linguistic sanctuary'
Jason Allen-Paisant

'Romalyn Ante's mesmeric new collection is deeply rooted in the dualities of life, cultural identity, and the profound interplay of personal and communal experience. Vivid, lyrical, and always surprising, it is a testament to those who navigate the complex legacies of history toward healing and resilience. It is both a balm and a call to action, reminding us of the transformative power of bearing witness'
Nathan Filer

'Romalyn Ante's first collection introduced us to a voice both vibrant and thoughtful. This collection grows out from this – now coming with a feeling of added power and forcefulness. This is a special book – both urgent and beautiful'
Niall Campbell

'With precision, deftness, and at times playfulness, *AGIMAT* weaves in mythical and modern imageries, the universal with the intimate. The result is a powerful and hopeful collection, filled with heart and beauty, that illuminates us to the many forms that caring and healing can take'
Cecile Pin

ALSO BY ROMALYN ANTE

Antiemetic for Homesickness

AGIMAT

Romalyn Ante

Chatto & Windus
LONDON

1 3 5 7 9 10 8 6 4 2

Chatto & Windus, an imprint of Vintage, is part of the Penguin
Random House group of companies whose addresses can be
found at global.penguinrandomhouse.com

Penguin
Random House
UK

First published in the UK by Chatto & Windus in 2024

penguin.co.uk/vintage

Typeset in 11/14pt Minion Pro by Jouve (UK), Milton Keynes
Printed and bound in Great Britain by Clays Ltd, Elcograf S.p.A.

The authorised representative in the EEA is Penguin Random House Ireland,
Morrison Chambers, 32 Nassau Street, Dublin D02 YH68

A CIP catalogue record for this book is available from the British Library

ISBN 9781784745776

Penguin Random House is committed to a sustainable future
for our business, our readers and our planet. This book is made
from Forest Stewardship Council® certified paper.

To my comrades in healthcare,
and to my 'children'.

For Suriya, as always.

Remembering is the best revenge.

                     —Maria Rosa Henson

Ako ang babaeng hindi matatakot
sa putok ng baril bala'y ganga niog.
Ako'y natamaan sa aking tugatog
pinispis ko lama't akala ko'y lamok.

        —Batangas folksong, E. Malabanan, 1916

I am a woman who is not afraid
of gunshots, bullets as big as coconuts.
Once, I was hit at the back of my head
I swept it away, thinking it was a mosquito.

[Evening walk, Wednesfield]

I navigate this light-pricked town;
my shadow skims on pavements –

rain-embossed leaves,
fox-eyed alleyways.

I reach the tunnel of tulle-purple fog
and my thoughts flicker like the canal waters.

As the hour deepens, I wonder how far
this heart can listen.

Mebuyan and Me

there is a season that mimics sucklings
a gust of laughter through the grating pendulum
of park swings
there is a weight to longing

a melody

a woman hums
her torso a towering bole
bronzed and swollen with burls
of breasts

nipples stout as pimpled bark
call a soul to crawl and suck

Mebuyan

isn't that her name
the goddess who rode in a giant rice mortar
spinning through the underworld

she lulls the children from *womb to tomb*
nightjars croon from the hollow
of her navel
as the moon lactates gloom-sweet sap

to salve every wound
cool the sting of snakebites
in the ankle or behind the knee

*

when the rowans combust in misery
we burst into a house on Guy Avenue
trace the sour grunt of a long-gone mum
curled on the penny-rust of a kitchen floor
in the crook of her elbow a needle glints

her toddler under the sink
we scooped him out
his stomach an unplugged drain churning
a torrent of tarnished nails

at home

where the soft-blue nightlight
paints birdhouses on the wall
I teach my nephew
to spell   *song*   and   *hope*
while other children shatter
like meteorites   learning a language
of anger and appetite

my nephew inks   O
over and over
a hungry mouth
an echoing wound
the paper breaks

During the pandemic, I tell my lover I can no
    longer be a nurse, and he writes 言霊 on my arm

Kototama – the magic that lives in words
like the feather of a rainbow inside smoky quartz,

or a glimmer of saline
in a thumb-sized, intravenous chamber.

Perhaps, this is the reason we shout,
                Open your eyes! like an invocation

every time we shake an unconscious man on the bed,
                on the pavement, on the passenger seat.

*

        言 for *words*, 霊 for *soul*.
I'm still waiting for the moon's light
to come upon me.

My lover says, *Don't quit*
and I wish he'd believe I want to persevere,
preserve what prayer is left

like that organ still playing
in a medieval church in Halsberstadt,
the music that will live for another 600 years.

But everything burns out:
the clocks of London, the Statue of Liberty
oxidized from copper to green.

*

In the dehydrated plateau
of my mother's hand, my kisses bloom
like silver puddles.

Yesterday my mother saw her pregnant patient
walk to the toilet with brick-
heavy breaths –

 on the way back, she collapsed –
 her yellow shawl falling with her
like mist over a forgotten mountain. The scan reveals

 thrombosis in the lungs, in the head,
snake eggs lodged in the arteries –

ᜅ᜔ᜊ

the curse of taking care of others

*

My lover says, *Try to find the same magic
in the language of your foremothers, Baybayin:*

the script colonisers tried to eradicate,
etched around the mouth of the Manunggul Jar.

ᜀᜂᜁ

which means *to spell*
or
seashore

The ⌒ is not a shell
but a woman's pelvis. It gives life to

ᗡ

shamaness
or
warning

*

I have sung all the love songs in the morgue

even before I sprint to my patient
trying to hang herself on the curtain rail.

It's already September
by the time I catch her by the legs.

Since then, I've been dreaming of my mother
dreaming of me

in the tachycardic pulse
of skeletal-white Resuscitation light.

We are running in slow motion,
our chests brown and blue fabrics torn open.

*

*Have you ever seen a person
shot in the head?* my mother asks.

That's how my patient dropped.
No leaning-on-the-wall

or breaking the body's collapse
with outstretched hands.

My mother and I sit in the deep-
green grass outside A&E, hurling curses

at the Sandwell skyline. Then laughing
at our paper cups of watery hot chocolate.

Is it wrong – to not want to claim misery
when everybody else is competing for it?

How the ⌒ breathes life to

ꙩꙩ꙰   *woman*

ꙩꙷ   *get up*

*

The garnet shade of dusk creeps down
the scribbles on my arm –

Kototama. *The magic that lives in words.*

But I have been blind, standing
in the blue flicker of my patient's television,

watching his favourite game show.
The black lakes of my pupils

singe, slates of scrambling letters on the screen:

M A P R I Y T R S O E

Can you see? my patient wheezes
under his oxygen mask.

The letters rearrange themselves to

a spirometry
or
try a poem, sir

How *breathless* bears
heart and *bless*

inhalation
hail and *nation* –

*

I am trying to leave this country.
I am trying to love this country.

The news says: *John Alagos,*
collapsed after a 12-hour shift . . .
My mother texts back: LOL

The news says: *Cases rising* . . .
Danger of nurses quitting . . .
My mother texts back: LOL

All this time my mother thought LOL
stands for *lots of love.*

*

My lover writes on my arm, kototama –
I have found my tribe though I am not brave enough
to sit around the campfire and memorise our song.

I cannot see that *respiratory*
breathes life to
repair and *story*

*

Is it wrong – that tomorrow as the ghost
of a star dilutes in the light of dawn

this body tattered and reverberating
will still get up,
will still work.

Will – the word we use to haul ourselves
to the valley yawning like a lion;

the word my mother and I fan with our palms
like a green flame

to defy this thunderstorm.
My lover warns me, *There is magic in words*

so be careful with what you say.
The full moon outside A&E

rising above the orbs of streetlights
on this ordinary October night

is surely beautiful,
but I just can't feel it anymore.

[In Transit]

Someone in the carriage shouts,
Chinks! Virus carriers!

Specks of gold upon black –
a lit skyline reels across my face

reflected on the train window
in a town that hasn't learned

to love us back.

Mebuyan teases Hermes

*'Being busy is . . . an attitude, a habit, and a value . . .
we are all in a hurry.'* – NURSING INQUIRY

Call that fast? Buick-quick? Lie
in the night clouds of your mama's quilt,

we're already elbow-greased. Listen:
my sister sings, recoils into a tokay gecko,

our ceiling winds with her creaks
like an old-fashioned alarm clock.

Malachite skin slips in and out of the thatching,
in the alleyways of work and sleep.

You ain't fast, you just hex women
(like that nymph too tired to attend your party)

into a lethargic drag –
turtle-shelled, a whole household on her back.

Don't you know, my mama's muscle
is made up of one million springtails.

She zigzags across the bay – from bed
to bed. The sheets she blindingly made.

How can the body generate such energy?
Some call it *duty*, some call it *love*.

My mama moves faster than a yellow balloon
exploding molecules of moonstone

your naked eyes cannot grasp. I slap
the back of a choking man, with the speed

of a mantis shrimp catapulting a mollusk
out of its shell. This

is how we work, Hermes. Swifter
than a frog's tongue-clutch. Here, I am sewing up

the wound from a Year 11's compass cut
whose prom was cancelled, whose father died

waiting for his cancer treatment.
No time to cry or sit in the funeral of crows.

Carry on, carry on. Lárga nang lárga.
We've inherited leafhopper-thighs,

our tendon splinters quick, our skeleton dries.
Can't you see: what you're looking at

is already pickled in the past. This black thread
holding the gash closed has already been tied tight.

Hermes, we're already miles ahead
way before you reach this line.

Mebuyan and the Golden Boot

the impacted fracture in the leg
of a young man who jumped
from a railway viaduct
is a hairline fault in the sky
tilted at forty-five degrees

these godly hands now desiccating
blistered and lesioned
tending to flowers that cannot contain
their own blossoming

maybe the mind mistranslates the world
still I want to find what beauty
is left in this quarantined town
only the rock-blue silence of blackbirds
the empty football ground seems wider than before

life is too short   or too long
depending on who is living it
the young man bawls
waking from the thin membrane of anaesthesia
when I ask for his date of birth he answers *June 24th*
same as Leonardo Messi's
My dog my family rescued from Ghana
The day I jumped off the bridge

this poem is a catalogue of what is missing
dopamine   serotonin   aprons
masks   gloves
his teammates racing through

the hamstrings of the wind
the green whir of dribble drills
the paisley wallpaper at the cafe
where they used to meet after each practice
to order chip butties

he says he is thirsty
he hoarded pills like hummingbird eggs
maybe the heart is lost between translations
the neurogenic-blue wings
flitting amongst flowers and thorns

life is a catalogue of hospital tasks
the young man says he is thirsty
but he swallowed all the hummingbird eggs
his heart is also a hummingbird

he tells me *This is how we live now*:
the new normal
even the man who knocks to deliver pizza
shields himself in the teal-acrylic dark
only the length of his arm
clutched by the porch light

en route to work I pause to gaze
at the lush rice terraces
of lichen on the boot of a footballer statue
outside Albion

my hands are desiccating
every week there is another hummingbird
dropping like a little rock

the footballer statue squints
at the metallic-pink edge of dawn
perhaps gauging how far the goal is
which translates as
how high the sky is
a mistranslation of
I am ever so sorry
for misjudging the kick

[Woden Road, after Work]

The robins roost along the cable lines
like speartips in an Old Master's canvas
of a nameless war. I hold my breath –
why can't I hear them sing?

My father asks why I date a Japanese man

We are stuck in traffic under Selfridges Bridge.
Father grips the steering wheel. *Don't you know
what the Japanese did to our country?* I know.
But memory is a swallow nest, fragile and shifting,
and love is a salamander skiing down white clouds
of window glass.

Hindi mo ba alam? Father doesn't move,
though the light's green, the cars behind in chorus, blaring.
He stares beyond the windshield – at hectares
of rice fields he ploughed as a child. His steel
clanks against another steel – half-buried,
crusted mortar bomb dropped at a time
when every window was blown to embers
that children mistook for fireflies.

*

My grand aunt in Cuenca: the night before she wed,
found two bombshells in the courtyard.
Thinking they were rocks, she set them as a stove
onto which the cooks laid their cauldrons.

Minced goat meat, sautéed onions.
Hiss. An explosion
of limbs.

Father scaled a tree to fetch
an arm dangling from a bough;
a ladle still clutched in its hand.

The map unfolds in front of Father's face –
a lieutenant asks him to translate
every cavern small enough to squeeze through.

The villagers say where darkness lies,
there are barrels brimming with Yamashita's gold.
Father says where darkness lies,
people console themselves with an imagined trove.

The lieutenant beckons an army truck,
tarps the area for three days –
even the crickets can't peek through.

Father tastes the bitter moss in his mouth,
grazes through tunnels small as rabbit holes,
emerges to the atomic flash of moonlight.

*

Father's uncles were force-fed
water through a hose.
There's a trellis in our old kitchen
chipped by the blades of Kempeitai
where they pinned Tio Nardo,
stabbed his stomach dry.

*

Bodies fill the Pamintahan well –
men, women, children.

A jeweller from Anilao excavates gold
teeth from the dead.

Some days I dream an omen:
a mountain ridge at bird's eye view –
the keloid scar on my grandfather's nape.
When he was young, a Kempetai kicked him

to his knees, thrust his head towards the well's mouth.
It was almost full – his face half-a-foot away
from a stomach erupting with blood.
When the soldier swung, he threw himself into the well,

feigning death. Others say he was already dead,
but opened his eyes when a scarab crawled into his ear.
The gash in his nape, blocked with pebbles and sand,
hardened into his body's talisman.

*

My grandfather, baptised Tagaliwás:
a guerrilla whose expertise was hit-and-run.

Tagaliwás: *protection from bullets,*
but also Tagâ: *hacked.*

Grenades bloomed in his pomelo tree.
Shrapnel like a meteor shower swerved from him

but a bullet hit the heart
of the woman he loved. Her chest burst

into the scarlet feathers of a macaw.
When birds cried outside his hut

he'd jump from sleep, trip in the shadow
of his blanket.

An invaded heart will swell
and suffocate in the body that houses it

until it splits open,
a pomelo doomed to rot.

*

The man I date is a Buddhist, confesses
he too was a soldier in his past life.

He takes my hand, across the metropolis
of Peri-Peri sauce bottles on the table,

lets me feel the birthmark in the jungle
of his gelled hair: his gunshot wound.

In this life, it is his talisman. I finger
the raised skin, the ridges of enemy lines,

before my father yanks my hand away
as if I am about to unearth something

long-buried, or pull the safety pin of a grenade.

[Lover's Bridge, Birmingham]

Padlocks cram the rails of Lover's Bridge –
an amalgamation of alloy and rust,
passion and penance.

A key thrown in the canal, a star
too many lightyears away to see.
Still there, nevertheless.

Spider Fight

In a thicket of leaves and limestone rocks,
we hide in the shade of an Ipil tree,
squatting deep, heads bent
to watch two spiders on a twig.

Yours has white stripes on her back,
scored by last night's lightning.
Mine is a nut of sun
that tickles the skin of my knuckles.

The whole forest stills
around the rumble of their legs
as they strike each other –
the impact makes both spiders fall,
hang mid-air on wind-lashed webs.

How many times yours bites mine
in the stomach – dots of blood
glow zircon-blue, like the worms
in bomb-shelter caves.

Yours grabs the orb of my little sun
with pedalling legs. A blast of light
from her spinneret cauls my spider
into a pearl, a sham amulet

that makes our shadows ripple
here at the heart of the woods.
We are salted with the knowledge
of what it's like for a life to be at stake.

When war arrives, something leaves
both quiet and bloodshed-loud.

Soon, we'll pivot to the sharp whistles
of our fathers from beyond the groves –
their stories about a Kempeitai
hiding in the bush, ready to slit
the throat of a wandering child.

We will run, abandoning
my little yellow sun
who is still scrambling –
one leg out of the silver strands,
tearing her way back
to this impossible life.

Haematology

Under the microscope,
my blood cells shift. These mauve,
biconcave discs are a battalion plodding
through a swamp. I adjust the knob and find,
in focus, my grandfather's brown iris – in his rifle's
scope. His inhalations synchronise with mine.
We breathe so slow, but unobscured. His eye
holds the shadow of a Kempeitai in loin-
high grass in which his ear is still intact,
his skull not yet a gorge of brain
and gore; not yet a tor
of scorpions.

I zoom in –
the Kempeitai moves
through a seaside town,
into a room with translucent
sheets on lattice frames, where
he stoops, mouth pursed
to the globe of his wife's
abdomen.

Grandfather blinks,
switches the slide – in which
his mother (and other mothers)
are still gorgeous, pounding clothes
by a brook, their groins not yet oozing
with knuckle-bruise, their newborns
not yet tossed skywards from
the mould of comfort
rooms

to be
almost-anointed
by a slash of light,
before being caught, impaled
on the Kempeitai's blade;
and now I cannot
look

[Beyond the Cut]

Meet me in that abandoned assembly line,
amongst littered bottles of wine: terrariums
filled with empires of moss and liverwort.

Meet me by that egg-blue wall, with a graffitied man
in a silver cap, pulling down the zip of his crotch –
the trajectory of his piss blasts into a thicket of red vines.

Comfort Women Diptych

A statue dedicated to Comfort Women who were raped and assaulted in wartime has been removed in the Philippines . . . Authorities may have removed the statue under Japanese pressure – United Press International, 2019.

Because a girl thrown in a well
will hoist herself back up.
Her dislocated limbs pointing
at the sharp margins of the wind
will clack back into their sockets.
She will cock her gaze
to the round sky, glaring at the god
bowing down to her.

Because the walls of the well
are calcified with white corals
scaling as far as she can see.
A body is a sculpture underwater.
The contusion in her left eye
pulses into a red starfish.
Algae radiate in the archipelago
of cigar burns on her thighs.

[First Date, Queen Square]

The statue of Prince Albert on the horse
is streaked with what seems to be
the frenzied dashes of fireflies

which is really a disco of little drones
you captured with a long-exposure lens
on the night that began our lifetime.

Hisashi

Bare tree trunks strum your name tonight,
I forget what Father preached:

that a woman must stay faithful to her books.
Instead, I count the sweat rhinestoned on your neck,

trail your dark blue hair on basketball courts,
stand on tiptoe to reach your sun-scarred brow

but never able to lay kisses on it.
What blurs the streetlights of Ladywell Walk?

The buzz of summer that must always end?
What pushes someone to beg, *Stay!* Onegāi –

your palm rubs my mosquitoed thigh,
your gaze beaming in a fastbreak of desires.

I vow not to look for our bubblegum-pink sky
or a comet's pearlesque arc overhead,

but soon I'll pass by a tatami shop,
stall at a snatch of your scent in the air.

A ball swishes through a net and I'll turn –
to find commuters spilling from Galton Bridge.

Though dusk has pawned our youth, I still walk on
searching for your hair dyed in chōchin lights

or that green whistle snugged between your lips.
Yet, you are a smoke that slips between my fingers.

A friend once said we yearn for the past,
exhausted by the load of our present.

Another street tilts to a rain-bright slope –
again, I baulk – baulk at the breeze,

once intimate and unafraid to bruise.

The Enchantress, at seventeen

(for grandaunt)

When a Kempeitai tears your underwear
and pinions you to the ground, his knees
on your shoulders, you clutch his scrotum
and pluck it like a bad fruit,

and when one pounces for your toddler
born out of their immortal loneliness
and tosses him into the ravine,
you howl a howl that, to this hour,
still echoes in the rocks.

They say your hands were strong
even before they came.
Now your fingers chafe
to the bare shine of knucklebones
as you dig for sweet potatoes
at the shelter cave;

you haul clay jars of water
from rivers in cobra-strangled woods.
The tilapia you catch with a bamboo spear
pelt themselves against the tin basin;
their glittering scales
sequin the soot of your footprints.

They say your hands were strong
even after they came.
Now you put two fingers between your lips,
to whistle for stray dogs, lay before them
a bowl of steamed fish.

Such strong hands.
You rub a dozen heads
that buzz with the reconnaissance
of flies, and burn with scabies.

Mebuyan peers at a food parcel from Zeus

What glints with thrushes' song? A can of beans,
four pimpled apples, one biscuit, two spuds.

A smorgasbord of naught, no goody greens –
no worms for the chicks, just a clump of mud.

Their copper chorus thrills the sky, too weak.
Rashford kicks and tweets – this isle is barren.

A maggot split for twenty-seven beaks? –
Why is it so mean? Ang bulók, Britain!

Who'd fuckin' think? Ketchup's a vegetable.
Count: one oxblood-bloom of peptic ulcer,

two bruised bananas croon on the table;
3 + 3's what? – drool until next summer.

The parent birds search for scraps in the soil.
Zeus withholds the worms, watches a banquet spoil.

[Saturday, at the entrance of Birmingham New Street]

Cigarette smoke rises into the air,
spectral, like a long-gone hurt,
suddenly resuscitated.

I look up at the top of the stairs
scanning for your face.
It never appears.

A Child Sent to Mebuyan's Clinic

Miss, I want to walk with Cody Drake in the corridors;
butt in like the others when he speaks of *Kane, Walker*:
those unfamiliar names that sound like heroes in folklore.

A white-tailed eagle sweeps the woods; I want to score –
whoosh that ball into infinity, like the *sickest striker*.
I want to laugh with Cody Drake along the corridors.

At home, I practise scissor kicks, knee-slide the floor,
utter *Wagwon? Bollocks* in front of the mirror;
the unfamiliar words bubble like potions of yore.

In my wallet, I stash Season cards from Singhsbury's store,
sub Jesus Christ with Kane surging for a header.
Our fist-bumps ripple red down the corridors.

But Cody calls me *gay*, flicks my ear till it's sore
since I trade Kane for *three freakin' mingers*;
their unfamiliar names, only sidekicks in this strange lore.

Yes, I nicked Nkosi's cards, called that grass Beth a *bore*.
I get it, Miss. Some vultures rip the sky in eagles' feathers.
But I want to laugh with Cody Drake in the corridors:
the lads to flock me – just once – to be the hero on this shore.

Upside Down

In this place, my father is *both* and *neither*,
an ambigram like the word *swims*

that still reads as *swims*, though upside down;
often drowning, but never dying.

At night, he escapes through the back door
to walk in the fragrance of this town:

through parks full of rowans, ultraviolet in the rain,
and the remnants of teenage lust,

while he – alone as a kicked, empty can,
considers what it means to be both at once.

I look at his old face and see a wheel-less bicycle
chained to a railing.

Sometimes he thinks he's still a bachelor,
(as if he was still in our old country)

strumming guitars for women the same age as I am.
To be or not to be, the question does not matter,

for he is that simple *yeah*, agreeing louder,
though grieving with a thousand *nos*,

passing through the life he was dealt –
harmonica blues blowing through a sidewalk

of littered crisp packets. Here, he waits
to be understood, and to understand,

impatiently patient as one waits
for the pedestrian lights to change,

Fang of Lightning

In Batangas, my father wears the pangíl ng kidlat;
it gives him healing powers:
he chiropracts dislocated bones,
his songs make the hemiplegic run,
the dying dance.

In Wolverhampton, he works at a care home
where a resident chucks his blue pills
into a fish bowl and strikes my father in the chest;
my father's ribcage is a village
collapsed by a distant-yet-deafening-war,
a church bell ringing over houses on fire.

My father's own breath: a reading
of scar-silvered chest scans,
clusters of gypsophilas at West Park.
He walks ten miles to car boots on Sundays,
picks up pennies in the car parks,
and augurs the labyrinth of ice crystals
on the feet of Lady Wulfrun in town.

When he finds another resident on the floor
still as a dead salmon, he swoops like a hawk,
and finger-swipes the dislodged dentures
out of his mouth. *Ganyan talaga*, he tells me.
Some people choke not on objects,
but on something we cannot name.

On his break, he spreads a blanket
on the Stock Room floor, lies on a space
as wide as a grave, where he can sail
in his five-minute sleep, a thunderstorm
breaking out under his eyelids.

His silence, an incantation.
His altar, an aftermath.

Mebuyan Meets Juan Tamad

This is your life, Juan Tamad,
you who sleep all day under a tree,
your lashes shudder under your wicker hat.

O Juan Tamad, remember that late September
your mother goaded you to the pond
to catch alimasag? You snipped the strings

that tied their claws shut, and asked the crabs
to crawl themselves back to your hut.
Your mother's scream stabs like lightning

but your body, your chest
is tougher than her cane.
There you go again, lying

under the tree, waiting for the guava to snap
off its stem, plummet into your open mouth.
Your mother taps the butt of your guitar,

Umawit ka, Juan! But you rub your wrists
heavier than monoliths; the soundhole
is the entrance to a colony of fire ants.

Juan, can't you hear the concerto
of the woodland macaques? The hornbills
circling above those drenched canopies?

Your mother snatches off your wicker hat,
kicks you at the ankle,
Look at that mountain, Juan! –

the Súso ng Dalaga, shape of a woman's breast,
teased by broken wisps of clouds. She says, *Get up!*
Life is beautiful! That mountain is beautiful!

And all day you wonder,
whose life?
Which mountain?

[Alone at the Sky Terrace]

From up here, the roads form a labyrinth
burnished in lava-gold street lamps.

The skyscrapers specked with radiance
buzz through the purple evening –

like an adagio that makes the heart twinge
for something that never happened.

Looking up at the 700-year-old tree inside
   Kayashima Station

Misted light diffuses through the canopy
of kusu no ki, the tree housing ai no kami.
Two claps and a congregation of warblers

erupt in strands of galactic green.
I bow to my pressed palms,
because everyone prays

for stupid stuff, like love.
But the gods in their sun-bleached robes
turn a blind eye. Some things

are too holy to be touched.
Kino-kun calls to me, *He likes you too!*
while making kissing sounds.

He doesn't know I've stopped praying for you
to turn around and pass me
my Physics paper, with a wink

that could pulverise the volt-blue stars
of Andromeda. I've stopped hoping
for an April that never arrives.

I close my eyes for a second
and the future's already a gate half-closed,
grating in the dust, siphoning sunset scraps

while a tannoy tears the shadows of peregrines,
announcing the approach of the Birmingham
train. You must know what it's like

to cut through the refracted colours
of commuters, weathered by rain
and their own unanswered prayers.

The iron horses along the tracks
endlessly gallop to rust.
And I – I'm still panting;

my head turning left
and right, scanning for the train,
not sure if it's yet to arrive

or has already gone.

Aegis

I stand amongst black fibulas of birches: a guarded woods or a hospital graveyard? The air spasms, mud regurgitates. My comrade entrusts a cobalt thread to me – a tap, and the tablet burdening my hands radiates with scanned scrapbooks – relics borne by nurses from the Great War.

One has gilded scripts eroding on its bark-brown sheath, embossed with abundant fleur-de-lis, the other leathered in blood-maroon. The wind picks up, sloughing the landscape's scabs. I swipe a leaf:

> *Time should be counted by heart-throbs . . .*

inked on Nurse Carter's jaundiced page. I know these are a poet's words, but this scribble – firm and funebrial – was signed by [undecipherable]phemia Brown.

Nurse Carter cradled her scrapbook to France, Salonica, Gallipoli and Egypt, escorting stricken soldiers home – her aegis engraved with patients' and allies' tales.

Can it be? No matter how dark, the night dilates; history a refrain I, too, must learn. Each dreamwaking thickens with sclerosis of grief. Crimson moon, a clot beyond barren branches, I tread on the soil's scar tissues, thickening into skeletal leaves.

Then BANG, a fever blaze, fallen fellow trunks. Crepitus of twigs. A hymn – pyretic and pale – I hear its name: *It's a Long Way to Tipperary*. Echoes of men. Epoch of tattered snow.

Once, my mother's Alzheimer patient battling the Delta variant suddenly hummed *Tipperary*. What, in the summons of survival, stirs?

Every night on the dark motorway, my mother and I drive home to Wolves. The beams a parallel of long quartz rutilated with rain.

Sometimes we wake to clanging pots and pans, palpitations in puddles – neighbours CLAP, CLAP, CLAP, convinced clamour celebrates us.

Streets are red with tippets –

pens Sister Dakin on Nurse Pearce's book. In Lincoln, a vast military hospital treated 45,000 men throughout the war.

We've a very happy time, she scribbles,
but if we stay here another year, we deserve the R.R.C.

In the frontline, we seek so little. My mother rolls people onto their stomachs for easier breathing – the weight shifts – the heart and other organs on the chest, not the lungs.

The darkest cloud has a
silver lining . . .
wear it inside out

signs Walter. Cliff. on June 18.

A crescent of sweat waxes on my mother's collar. Cardiac flutter in ferns. Crickets' syncope.

Wounded 12th of July near Neuve Chapelle

records Private Bond of the 12th(?) Sherwood Foresters for Nurse Blythe-Brown.

tryed to stop a shell, but the shell stopped me.

Nebulised rain stings my eyes. Marbled arteries of light.

Should I give up or carry on? Sometimes, the song tells of a clearing – a dawn's blue thorax, where stars are more than just a tally. BANG, BANG, BOOM, BOOM.

In my clinic, my colleague knocks, informs me,

One of your children relapsed.
Their mother just phoned.

Mothering other mothers' loves, my finger traces impulsive cuts – narratives on skin; my hands bandage another lash – sharp chlorhexidine. The scrapbooks flicker into Inpatient folders. Flowers in a purple dell, thick, susurrus like sores.

I am no longer young,
sadder but not wiser . . .

Vera Brittain writes in the book my mother gifts me.

my experiences have taken me far
beyond those . . . of my contemporaries.

Lost in these woods, how much more to lose when loss is not surrendering but a heavying.

I want to pose my arm, tense my deltoid muscle like Rosie the Riveter or my Instagram friends flaunting a little plaster, proof of vaccination. I want to say so easily – *I did my part*, but stranger plains await. I've yet to take anything; I've only learnt giving up.

I stoop to check a thigh – a flapped wound – pale orange flesh heaving like a young bird's feathered skull breaking out of its shell.

In the corridor, my comrade and I cross. Masked, we nod, but do not chat.

[Iron Bridge]

Two people stand still on the Iron Bridge –
a mother-and-daughter, or, maybe, best friends.

But only one woman's silhouette reflects on the Severn,
the other one, a sun's lucent stamp on water.

Agimat

A child bears many faces, but mine
was overcome by the panic of dusk.
So my father chanted, transplanting
a spell to my blood. Agimat ko
hiningáng-bugá sa aking noó.

*

Soon, I stopped recoiling from the bark
of the next-door Dobermann. I whistled,
strolling past metacarpal twigs
that scraped into Kapre's hands.

Father sang, *Lahat may Agimat.*
Everyone has Agimat. Passed down
to every child: this charms the buried light of stars –
this deflects bullets – this unblooms a war –

*

But I've forgotten all the trees of our town.
How once, astride a branch, I coaxed god
to come down – with ginger lilies
steeped in Agimat,
plucked from the rib of a precipice.

*

My clinic's walls throb,
soil in the rain.

In this swivel chair, I gasp
but I can't drown
every time a child knocks,
Nurse, I cut myself again.

He rolls up his sleeve –
dried herringbone of scars.
In the season of arachnids,
a Year 9 leaped off a cliff,
believing her shadow dragged
the red-granite wind.

*

Nurse, in my hometown, sunrise blasts
like gunpowder; twilight sizzles
with fragments of flesh.

I laid dried dates onto my father's plate,
filled oil jars with copper coins
I earned from brushing factory rugs.

His only Agimat, gold motes
rising to his face.

*

Nurse, I took a peek –
Father furs into a wild boar,
meth-bright tusk
stabs Mother at her cheek.

ᜊ ᜍ ᜎᜓ ᜆᜒ.
ᜍᜒᜊᜒ ᜎ ᜊᜒ
ᜊᜍᜓ ᜍᜍ ᜏ
ᜈᜊᜒ ᜏᜍᜈ

ᜊ ᜊᜒ ᜈᜈᜍ
ᜆ ᜊᜍᜒᜍ ᜎ ᜎᜈ
ᜆ — ᜊᜒ ᜍᜍᜈ
ᜍᜍᜎ ᜈᜆ ᜈᜊ

Last night a mound of laundry swelled
into wreckage. My father's hand poked out,
asterisked with black powder and blood.

*

There is a place where grazed knees
and elbow wounds become bearable –
where a child crawls
out of the bruises of a field
into a dusk so lustrous
heaven marinates itself.

*

I will rehearse the Agimat-bearer's chant
until a child can sleep in its lullaby

of unearthed skulls,
a spine glowing like a tower
in a rain-swept town.

*

May this clinic tremor into a cave
vines swallowing the door beams,
a burl that encrusts the knob –
I will chant until every wound
seals, and no child knocks,
Nurse, I cut myself again,
and a girl will be unbreakable
as she leaps into the wind.

The Sama-Sellang

Have you heard of them? The clan of women who dip their fingers
in the ocean to scan a typhoon's trajectory, the contusions
of rainclouds? Once, I found the shadow of my grandmother bobbing
in the bow of her boat. Her hands in motion – a conductress
directing the turns of surf. When the mist thinned,
I realised she was hauling a net – the ropes invisible in the distance.

My ear leans to the waves, to the turmeric-tinge of sand
imprinted with the arrivals of fishermen: fingers blasted,
blood seeping through gauzed arms. Many times our village wakes
to explosions: obelisk-white upsurges, concentric ripples.
Boomerangs of light shredding a thirty-foot radius.

And since we hear only the swell of malignant sun,
brined hands funneling white powder into empty bottles.
If god were a healer looking down, he'd see a cloud of embolism
on the earth's obsidian scan. He'd click his tongue –
our clan is gone. No finger-dip can halt a tsunami,
no hand-beat can subside or raise the tides.

Say it. We've been having the same dream:
some nights, we drift in the hum of a sunken ship as if light
were sacred again. Deck stairs stuccoed with corals that glint
copper coins and carnelian quartz. A mainmast branches
into purple staghorn, speckled at the tips with silver fish.

We've lived in those depths – where turquoise tides convulse
from the pneumatic bark of a dugong, sucking seagrass
above the seafloor-folds; where shrapnel withdraws
from fish flesh, the barracudas unbury their heads
from the ashen reef, and stelae of spiked fins start to flip.

Mebuyan's Song: Why is it Dark at Night

THE SCIENTIST:
There are more stars than grains of sand,
but they fall away when the universe expands,
so we'll never reach their light.

THE GRANDMOTHER.
There was once a poet who fell in love with a shinobi –
he hurled his kunai, conjuring a hundred lightning storms,
so she spilled her ink across the scroll of sky.

> REFRAIN:
> *Why are you out on this dark night?*
> *Come back home, out of wild beasts' sight.*

THE VILLAGE DRUNK:
Everyone I love has left.
I batter heaven with an empty bottle
until it shines in bruises.

THE VILLAGE PRIEST:
Everyone who's left, I've learnt to love.
My prayers flutter into blue-black moths
petalling around God's mouth.

> REFRAIN:
> *Why are you out on this dark night?*
> *Come back home, out of wild beasts' sight.*

MEBUYAN:
The food vendor on the pavement shoos away a street kid
with a rattan rod topped with a red plastic mop
she uses to shoo away flies.
She churns a broth of ox bone –

FOOD VENDOR:
This is the tastiest in town! When the crickets
stroke a chorus, this broth congeals into a moon
so luminous Queen Cosmos shuts her eyes.

REFRAIN:
Why are you out on this dark night?
Come back home, out of wild beasts' sight.

MEBUYAN:
Meanwhile, the child shooed away by the vendor,
accused of stealing by the priest, and punched in the eye
by her drunk father, walks out of an alleyway –
her silhouette between buildings, a semicolon;
she strolls the village alone, not finding out the truth

which is, that the gods and the kings,
in tales and histories, were all afraid of a child.
So they concocted a plan: they called up the dark,
smudged the world with the grit of their palms.

REFRAIN:
Why are you out on this dark night?
Come back home, out of wild beasts' sight.

MEBUYAN:
But no one calls the child home.
She hears nothing but the slantwise sheen
of scars on her arm.
The sky sinking darker now –
all pulverised glass of stars
falling further from her reach.
The wind flinches at the blades of leaves.
In some versions, the child grows up
to tell this story.

Captured

The class ruptures in screams
as an army of frogs leaps over the jar's brim.

Sir says, *Do it*. My small hands are quick to grab –
its webbed toes flick and twitch in an attempt to flee.

But Sir is quick to needle the top of its head
and stir the silver steel until it is dazed,

the see-through layers on its eyes
which Sir calls *nictitating membranes* sweep up

and down. We pin its palms onto the board,
and pinch below the stomach to make a cut –

from its abdomen up to its pulsing throat.
We forcep its mottled skin aside

to reveal the pink, beating flesh;
its lungs inflate full as balloon vines.

Searching for the heart, we slit once more,
raking the layers of its guts –

the sapphire cabochon of a gallbladder,
the supernova of unfertilised yellow eggs.

No wonder we are lonely now,
following orders without understanding why –

Highschool-Crush Haibun

'Mirror Flower, Water Moon' – JAPANESE SAYING

After your basketball training, you cross the town alone, dribbling along the pavement, making dust tremble copper. I trail in the wake of your shadow like the ghost of a plastic bag in a treetop. You reach the torri gate's shrine-red gleam, lights graze the loom of your back.

The sidewalk rows of sakura surrender fragrance as stall-shutters thunder to the ground. Reel me in your scent – my pleated skirt flaps in the wind and the surging Yuigahama waves in the east are electric with bioluminescent planktons. Once, you pause to watch it; my shadow eclipses your face, you blurt how much you love that sea: *Plain or pretty!*

Once, our paths cross at the torri gate, I side-glance at you side-glancing at me before our gaze drops back to our feet.

The road stretches on.
A jade-white moon hexagoned
in bright, linking clouds.

Mebuyan faces Lumabat

Brother, in this version, you are the Head
of the Underworld Primary – a perfect fit –

for at one year old, you started speaking
the poetics of slugs and frogs.

Today, one of my children came knocking,
crouched in the shadows of your voice.

He wept, ensnared by the thought
he couldn't wrap his head around anything.

All morning he leaned on the playground maple tree,
trying to wrap his head around it.

His neck strained, his head tilting like a little planet
perforated with light,

but only blonde strands got stuck on the black trunk
like streaks of racing, underworld hounds.

I can't! I can't do it, Miss!
he cried on the last school trip to Dudley Zoo,

wailing for the turaco he thought he must strike.
That is how he sees it, brother,

when you asked him to *hit two birds with one stone* –
now his palm is indented, a scar in the centre

the size of a blackhole
through which no one can peek but you.

Brother, how hard is it to say what we really mean?
When you shout, *You have your head in the clouds!*

he believes he will suffocate in their slate up-swirl.
At playtime, he digs his nails into his skin,

checking if he's turning into a vegetable
after you call him *beet-red.*

The class' laughter is a ricochet of fireworks
but his brain is an octopus

stretching its tentacles
like a carnival mime touching invisible glass.

Brother, these children are like me
when I first came to the Underworld.

In a college café of shuddering crypts,
a handsome skeleton swaggered to my table

and asked, *What are you doing?*
I replied, *Nothing, just sitting.*

Later, while looking in the mirror,
the coalpits of my eyes echoed

with the crawl of centipedes –
I realised what he was asking

was what *course* was I taking.
Migrants of the land, migrants of the mind:

torqued in someone else's thought-tongue.
Literalness, a kinship entwined.

No one wants the truth, but the formulated answer.
Ignoring my words, you munch on your ogre sandwich.

A piece of rocket clinging to your collar
coils into a chameleon. You wipe your mouth.

You have a more important meeting to attend.
A child is too big for the size of a language –

so I watch you, brother, as you dash
through the double doors,

straight to your car parked beside the graveyard
of sunflowers where it was bright and glowing,

but it's now raining cats and dogs.
Meow. Thump.

[M45]

Earlier at the clinic,
a child told me he wanted to drink bleach;
certain he *will never be healed.*

Driving on a fog-smothered road,
I cry over the sudden blossoming
of snowflakes on my windshield.

Half-dangerous

With the language that I know, love,
I carry you like this little rock
in my breast pocket.

Sharpness I cannot name –
no matter how long we live
from regrets to regrets.

Every night, a glass is half-empty-
half-full. This scarlet face half-wild
with what we are half-afraid to lose.

Your eyes – monitor-bright this morning
when you said you'd visit me.
I can almost see

you quivering into grey,
into wind, in all that is full
mooned in this city – the coral mist

over St Paul's dome – the orchestra
of bulbs outside Harrods.
What are you now but a vein

of alcohol in the throat –
this thread's breadth, almost-dangerous
distance between us –

seeing you may half-happen,
like the different languages
we try to speak. Like your mouth

that still cannot give an honorific
for the one you love the most.
You tell me about your foxgloves forest,

while I go on living, wandering
well-worn paths – past the neon red lights
rippling vertically on the Thames,

engulfing myself in the half-failing,
half-winning hum of the underground.
This city I dream – where you

are half-actual; this city you dream – fully
open and working now,
and still half-broken.

[Station Platform]

This morning of anticipation
calms in the blend
of lavender and patchouli,
humming on your neck;

we console each other
as I lean onto your shoulder,
here in the trick-play of silhouettes
and platform lights.

Love consumed is not lost
but loaned. Tiny as it is,
it is kept, until our paths,
once again, cross.

Mebuyan and the Pronoun It

I try to understand the syntax
of chance. What floods in through the gap
underneath this clinic door

but the tremble of light itself:
platelet pale, rising
inch by inch to my ankles.

A lancet
of sun cuts across her face: *I will get*
rid of it in Birmingham.

The pronoun now out of place,
no matter how desired by others, no matter how heavy
the rhododendrons bloom in May.

This morning, my toilet walls blew
migraine-bright, another pink line
ghosted by its twin in the result window

and the clouds descend in the cry of skylarks.
I will take
tablets, then I will bleed.

How words can be so metered and clear –
to have something
so as not to have *it*.

What can I do but be the breeze
that moves, lulling the flowers?
I wish I could tell her: in my dreams,

I'm always looking for *it*.
I hoist the weight of its shape
until its soft mouth latches on my breast.

But what can the breeze do but dissipate
between blossoms and leaves,
without looking down

at the swoop of discarded petals.

Mebuyan uses Cerridwen's Cauldron

This time, she asks the cauldron
if she'll ever be like Cerridwen, with a child to chase
through the woods, who shapeshifts into a ram or a goat.
Mebuyan wonders what she will name her young –

perhaps Mutya for *jewel* or Buhawi for *waterspout*.
She'll choose a name as sweet as the cherry blossoms
in the land of her father, or something that means
ocean or *born in summer*; those clumps of consonants

like balls of sticky rice that appease the spirits
on Hungry Ghost nights. On Fridays here, her child
will feast on battered fish and chips, and know
that faggots go best with peas. How a name carries

her ancestors' faces; its absence hurts her entire clan.
Mebuyan hears Cerridwen's children burst into laughter
from the carmine heart of the woods, but she does not
take her eyes off the water – now silvering into the wing

mirror of her car, parked outside the primary school
on Woden Road, where she waits for her sisters
to come out through the titanium gates
amongst the mass of other mothers, fathers, overflowing,

hand in hand with their little ones – *me Bab*,
a girl with tufted hair puts on a brown bear bonnet.
Another mother shouts for her boy
dashing on and off the pavement on his bicycle –

the red scarf at his neck fluttering like a carp kite,
until it drops at the barrage of car horns
and punctured gasps. The mother screams again,
I said to keep off the road! Right now, Jacob!

And Mebuyan asks the cauldron
if she'll ever have that voice, like an arrow
that pierces through the flesh of the afternoon,
calling a name with so much anger and love.

[Daily Run at Northycote Farm]

The noon sun taps me on my shoulder –
I look back to a burst of dandelion seeds
heading nowhere.

Magatama

This pale green jade from you, love,
hangs close; its polished curves
with patches of turquoise

glisten – sharp water
overcoming the shore,
wind incising tides.

May this pendant live on –
an heirloom in waiting,
if luck is on our side.

I wake up from a dream
to a midnight thunderstorm.
The magatama on my chest –

a waxing moon, a comma.
Shared breath
that fills the space

at our dinner table.
Beyond the waves
where selves are lost,

the Itoigawa Coast appears;
its shore a mosaic of blue and green.
There our future child –

bright-faced – plays, laughs,
as she picks up pebbles
scattered like syllables.

Breathe

I want to fly from the Black Country to Batangas,
rewind the honeyed scrolls of clouds
to search for the fang left by a lightning strike –

an amulet that will keep me alive.
But there is bracken of scar
flashing opalesque in my left lung.

In Respiratory class, we learned
that the right lung is shorter
because of the liver beneath,

the left narrower
as it shares room with the heart –
but what I love I can no longer breathe,

and the cold air of my new home
shreds like a quartz-
blue blizzard, like wolves circling their prey.

*

My consultant warns me, *Keep the mucus uninfected
and you can have a normal life
expectancy.*

> On my Obs rounds I keep
> my middle and ring fingertips
> on my patient Eduardo's wrist

pretending I'm palpating his pulse
when I'm tallying the rise
and fall of his chest.

An average person takes 8.4
million breaths a year. If we miss one
anong ala-álang malilimútan?

There are 600 million alveoli in the lungs.
Imagine your chest like a fire opal trance,
a symphony of wind-blown leaves.

In CPR, I give two breaths
for each cycle of compression –
what comes out of my lungs is life.

What's inside is decay – a mosaic of rot
colonising a bough, like the ruins of a war
my mother speaks of in another tongue.

*

I curl my palm into a cup, tap
the lower lobes of Eduardo's back.
Each seed of sweat is a point of light

that reflects a different version of myself –
healer or *patient*
migrant or *resident*

Tonight, the citrine-glow of Clarithromycin
primes his intravenous line – flushes sharp
into his vein. Tomorrow, into mine.

*

The hospital hallway dilates
I'm wheeling Eduardo but we're not moving –
only the mucus-green walls sweeping by.

I look down and I am the patient gasping
under a mask, fogged
with white breath-wreath of asters.

In Batangas, you once wrote to me,
We are gazing at the same stars
but seeing different constellations.

Depending on how you read it,

ᜋᜋᜓ

is *to love* or *to sob*

ᜎᜒ

is *ember* or *lungs*

*

I curl my palm into a cup, tap
the lower lobes of my back.
Each globule of sweat holds
a different version of the Odyssey.

Waiting for the O₂ Sats latched on my finger
like a Venus flytrap,
I watch the bioluminescent blue bars pump up.

I wheeze and wheeze –
the voices of my consultant, my patients, my mother
blur into cantatas dispersing through autumn hills.

        Waiting for the O₂ Sats
        latched on Eduardo's finger
        like a flytrap suffocating a lizard,

        I watch the bioluminescent blue bars pump up.
        I squeeze and squeeze
        Salbutamol into his nebuliser,

but I am the one leaning forward
to suck the mouthpiece.
Depending on when I face the mirror, I am

          healer or *patient*
            poet or *dumb*

The air that is me rests in nameless trees,
shifts the viscous leaves. Once, you and I laid with easy lungs
under the electric-blue waves of kingfishers in flight –

          ꑘꂷꀄꒉ

        is *lover* or *friend*

          ꀕꇞ

        is *reside* or *leftover*

              *

The most oxygen I can give
without the doctor's prescription
is ten litres per minute.

I can decrease it,
like how I titrate the dusk
by turning on the lamps.

Like how the gods choose
who is to breathe fully,
and who is to beg.

*

No other organ in the body can float in water
but the lungs: because the lungs are a pair of lifebuoys.
No other organ in the body can drown like the lungs,

(saltwater-burn of tissue, lacerating gasps)
because the lungs contain the breath of a lover,
the laughter of a patient, the myths of a mother.

When Zeus flooded the earth
to drown the warring men,
Astraea was so breathless

all she wanted was to be a star
oblivious that her own tears
helped swell the flood.

I refuse to sob.

Only this: an abrasion of wind
in my ribcage – a spill
of the milky way.

A constellation blinks
into mere needle pricks
on my left wrist.

*

I want to be at home, in this breath,
even on my death-breath days,
when I can find the blurred face

of my mother.
Tornadoes of embers
over our childhood campfire.

Between this breath and I,
God floats
in a mote of pollen.

*

My consultant gave me
a diagnosis, and I want to believe
the universe is just a set of coincidences. And it is

a coincidence that my lungs are collapsing
galaxies – and it is a coincidence
that the person reading this poem

is breathing fully.
The hallway's throat constricts –
the cup's orifice shrinks –

*

Eduardo sniffs the flower in a pot
for the last time. He still believes
something beautiful can emerge

from its own quiet tending.
Live life, so we try.
I can forever cannulate the tiniest veins,

we can forever laugh at Kierkegaard's
views on love, the camouflage of hearts.
Choking but alive.

ᴜᴦᴜꞵ

means *to hand over* or *bruise*

*

Eduardo and I – we're the same:
the life in our lungs is going out
faster than it goes in,

sometimes clogged, sometimes blurred,
like sea-spray on the face
on that once erratic boat ride.

What goes out is gone.
What we long for does not come back.
Like that island I was willing to lose sight of,

and the million miles of impossible-blue sky
I cannot breathe in,
I cannot cross back.

[Rendezvous at West Park]

Alone together, we gaze
at the sky swirling viscous
like water in a jar of blue glitter.

We insist on this hunger,
the way the glow-in-the-dark hands
of your watch penetrate the mist.

Touchstone teaches Mebuyan

Oh Noble Fool! A Worthy Fool! – As You Like It

They say a sculpture has done its work
when someone else imitates its pose.

Look at me, the Jester on Henley Street,
balancing on one patina-green foot,

the other, poised in the air.
But aren't we all on the brink of toppling over –

teetering on a life that is forever shifting.
Move and everything else moves with you

like the vibration of a helicopter above
in this June-clear sky, the heat-shimmer of laughter

of someone you love from afar.
Yesterday, a tamarind husk crumbled in your hand,

spilling all caught light. Today, your shadow clots
in a meadow of poppies spreading like fire.

Look – I am struggling or, maybe, feinting fun.
Enjoy comes from *une joie,*

'to make it a part of yourself'. You know this place,
you've learned the names of these streets.

Every day hundreds of tourists extend
their selfie sticks, copying my pose –

they want *joy* to be a part of themselves.
They seek happiness in this lopsided world, knowing

it is only the ground that keeps us aloft.

To my nephew who downloads games on
my phone

I'll teach you to fight, Tita Neneng,
he says, thumbing the screen,
his face, profound-blue.

Look, Tita Neneng, he spins the glass,
flicks a Pokeball to catch Jigglypuff
sets her to bounce beside my avatar –

a girl in a green parka,
a green beanie. *Green*
your favourite, Tita Neneng.

He types a name to my avatar,
loud as the growth of grass.
T-i-t-a N-e-n-e-n-g

Tita: *aunt*;
Neneng: *little girl*;
as all aunties were children too.

How I wish all aunties
retained the spirit of their nephews,
sure as the sun, the abundance
of tulips in Northycote.

Children swarm the schoolgate,
hugging each other in autumn's baritone,
as if we weren't told *Keep your Distance*
or *Stay Home* just last month.

I envy his ingenuity:
This Pokémon is a Fire type,
good against Steel, vulnerable to Rock.

I envy his courage
when in the middle of the night
he writhes, cupping his abdomen.

The nurse says, *It's protocol.*
So his mother goes in
and I stand outside
in the brisk October wind.

The skateboard park across,
an empty palace of asphalt –
no wheels crashing,
no heads down on phones,
as they walk hunting for Pikachu.

My pocket vibrates, a Pokémon
notification bell twinkling:
You can do it, Tita Neneng!
Who would not be moved
by such a pulse from a little thing.

[Best of Both]

Depending on the angle of light,

the Red Lion's broken windows
gleam like Laiya's peacock pearls;

the shade of Edwardian terrace houses
shifts in the depths of flame seashells.

Fire Flower

A stark-yellow speck
in a civilisation
of moss at my feet.

You have grown amongst
feldspar and graphite,
a jasper-glint of stem,

five millimeters
of amber buds –
How can I take care of you?

I think of my husband
whose irises, I now realise,
are not obsidian but kobicha-brown.

Love takes endurance –
we have tried and tried again.
Now this fire flower

rises to one-fifth of a thumb.
You do not even know
I am here.

This flame-gold splinter
radiates at my feet.
I am scared.

You are so dainty,
so scarce,
so breakable by breath.

Notes

During the pandemic, I tell my lover I can no longer be a nurse, and he writes 言霊 on my arm: The phrase 'Danger of nurses quitting . . .' is from the article 'Danger of nurses quitting after Covid-19 if mental health overlooked' (*Nursing Times*, 2020).

Comfort Women Diptych: The epigraph is from the article 'Statue dedicated to "comfort women" removed in the Philippines' by E. Shim (*United Press International*, 2019).

Mebuyan teases Hermes: The epigraph is from the article, 'Nurses' experiences of busyness in their daily work' by L. Govasli and B. Solvoll (*Nursing Inquiry*, 2020).

Mebuyan peers at a food parcel from Zeus: The italicised lines are from the news article 'Free school meals: Mother's "sadness" at "mean" food parcel' (BBC NEWS, 2021) and 'Profit in the pandemic: School meal rip-off' (*Russell Brand Youtube Channel*, 2021).

Hisashi: Hisashi is one of the characters in the Anime, *Slam Dunk*. In Japanese, the name also means 'a long time ago'.

Mebuyan Meets Juan Tamad: Juan Tamad is a character in Filipino folklore notorious for his laziness. Fatigue is a symptom in over 90% of depression patients. Before diagnosis, children and adolescents are frequently mischaracterised as lazy (*PsychCentral*, 2021).

Aegis: The scrapbook excerpts are borrowed from the *Service Scrapbooks: Nursing and Storytelling in the First World War* and can be accessed on the Royal College of Nursing's (RCN) website. The scrapbooks were owned by nine nurses and one Voluntary Aid Detachment. I thank Sarah Chaney, from the RCN, for leading me to these powerful artefacts.

Agimat: The incantation written in Baybayin script consists of two tanaga, an indigenous seven-syllable, rhyming, Filipino poetic form. The tanaga, predominantly passed down through oral tradition, embodies proverbial expressions, moral wisdom, and ethical precepts. The incantation in this poem was written to be sung, and has a guitar chord structure of C, Am, F, and G.

Mebuyan's Song: Why is it Dark at Night: This poem is written in the old Tagalog folk song form, talingdaw. The refrain has a guitar chord structure of G, Am, D. I thank my father for putting music to my words here and in the incantation from 'Agimat'.

Touchstone Teaches Mebuyan: This poem was written during my appointment as Shakespeare's Birthplace Trust/Hosking Houses Poet-in-Residence in Stratford-upon-Avon in 2019. I thank Dr Paul Edmondson for our conversation which inspired me to write this poem.

The Baybayin script in the poems 'During the pandemic', 'Agimat' and 'Breathe' is given in its traditional, pre-Hispanic form.

Acknowledgements

Deepest gratitude to the editors of the following magazines and anthologies that have welcomed my work into their pages: *Harper's Bazaar, Poetry London, Poetry Birmingham Literary Journal, Magma, Times Literary Supplement, Out of Time: Poetry from the Climate Emergency* (Valley Press).

I am indebted to the Jerwood Compton Fellowship for their unwavering support, without which the genesis of this book would not have been possible. A special mention of appreciation to Fiona Benson whose encouragement and guidance have been priceless on this journey.

I also thank the Society of Authors for the Arthur Welton Award, which allowed completion of this work.

I am forever grateful for the A-team at Chatto & Windus, particularly Clara, Rosanna and Priya, and above all, to my editor, Sarah, whose insights and dedication have been a tremendous help to this book.

To Isobel and Finlay at the Blakefriedmann Literary Agency, thank you for your ongoing support and advocacy.

Thank you, Mum and Dad. And of course, Suriya – your inspiration and boundless love have sustained me. To our baby dogs, Tia & Jiraiya, thank you for the walks and moments of joy. This book is dedicated most especially to our precious Selena-Rose.